ROMAN BRITAIN

Ruth Brocklehurst

Designed by Stephen Wright

Illustrated by Giacinto Gaudenzi

Edited by Jane Chisholm

Consultant: Dr. Andrew Gardner
School of History and Archaeology, Cardiff University

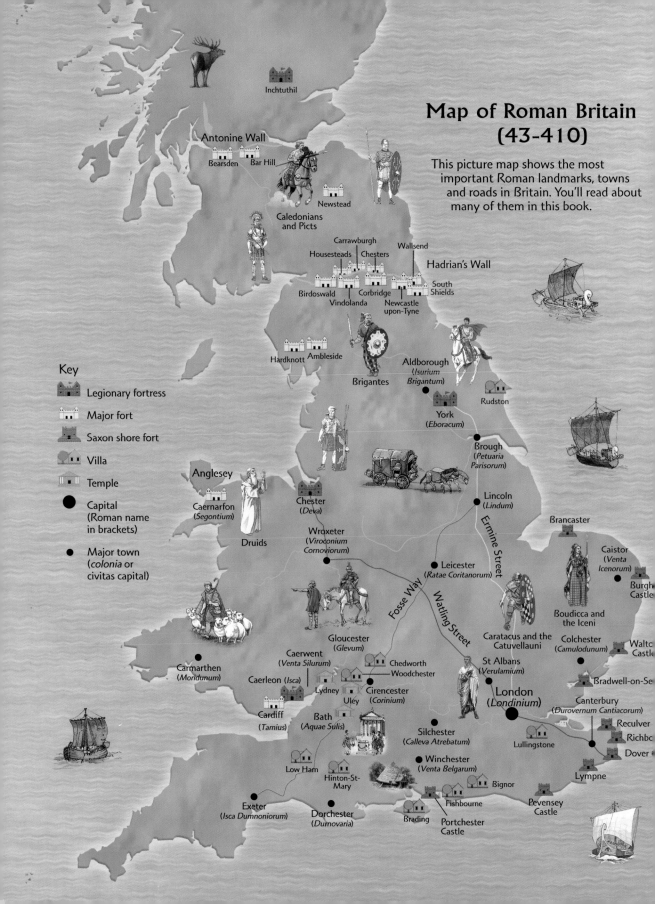

Map of Roman Britain (43-410)

This picture map shows the most important Roman landmarks, towns and roads in Britain. You'll read about many of them in this book.

Inchtuthil

Antonine Wall

Bearsden   Bar Hill

Newstead

Caledonians and Picts

Carrawburgh

Housesteads   Chesters   Wallsend

Hadrian's Wall

Birdoswald   Corbridge   South Shields

Vindolanda   Newcastle upon-Tyne

Hardknott   Ambleside

Brigantes

Aldborough
(Isurium Brigantum)

Rudston

York
(Eboracum)

Brough
(Petuaria Parisorum)

Anglesey

Caernarfon
(Segontium)

Druids

Chester
(Deva)

Wroxeter
(Viroconium Cornoviorum)

Lincoln
(Lindum)

Brancaster

Ermine Street

Leicester
(Ratae Coritanorum)

Caistor
(Venta Icenorum)

Burgh Castle

Boudicca and the Iceni

Caratacus and the Catuvellauni

Colchester
(Camulodunum)

Walton Castle

Key

Legionary fortress

Major fort

Saxon shore fort

Villa

Temple

Capital (Roman name in brackets)

Major town (*colonia* or *civitas* capital)

Carmarthen
(Moridunum)

Gloucester
(Glevum)

Caerwent
(Venta Silurum)

Chedworth

Woodchester

Caerleon (Isca)

Lydney

Uley

Cirencester
(Corinium)

St Albans
(Verulamium)

Bradwell-on-Sea

London
(Londinium)

Canterbury
(Durovernum Cantiacorum)

Cardiff
(Tamius)

Bath
(Aquae Sulis)

Silchester
(Calleva Atrebatum)

Lullingstone

Reculver

Richborough

Dover

Low Ham

Hinton-St-Mary

Winchester
(Venta Belgarum)

Bignor

Lympne

Exeter
(Isca Dumnoniorum)

Dorchester
(Durnovaria)

Brading

Fishbourne

Portchester Castle

Pevensey Castle

CONTENTS

Dates

Some of the dates at the beginning of this book are from the time before the birth of Christ. They are shown by the letters BC. Dates in this period are counted backwards.

Internet links

Look for the Internet links throughout this book. These are descriptions of websites where you can find out more about Roman Britain. For a link to these websites, go to **www.usborne-quicklinks.com** and type in the keywords "Roman Britain".

This man is dressed in the uniform of a Roman army officer.

ROMANS INVADE

Roman civilization began around 3,000 years ago, when a tribe called the Latins settled in Italy and founded the magnificent city of Rome. The Romans built up a powerful army and conquered many lands, until they ruled over the biggest empire of ancient times. Then, around 2,000 years ago, they set their sights on a small group of islands in the North Sea, which they called *Britannia*.

Imperial expansion

By 60BC – when the great Roman army general Julius Caesar rose to fame – the Romans dominated the Mediterranean region, from the Spanish Pyrenees, to the deserts of North Africa and Syria. In the lands beyond Italy, known as the provinces, the Romans imposed not only their laws and their hefty taxes, but also their way of life and their language, Latin.

This map, based on one from the 2nd century, shows what the Romans thought the British isles looked like.

HIBERNIA
(Ireland)

CALEDO
(Scotlar

BRITANNIA

In 58BC, Caesar and his troops were fighting to secure the Roman province of *Gaul* (France). Britain lay tantalizingly close, on what many Romans believed to be the very edge of the world. To capture these lands would surely be to conquer the world – or so they thought.

But Caesar had practical motives too. Some southern Britons were supporting Gallic rebels in their fight against Rome, and Britain was reported to be rich in gold and silver. To conquer both Britain and Gaul would be a tremendous boost to his career.

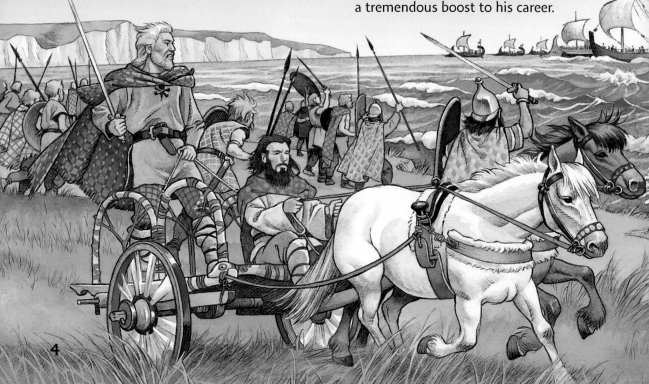

Painted barbarians

The Romans saw the tribesmen of Britain as barbarians – often drunk and always fighting. In battle, the Britons fought bare-chested, sometimes naked, with lime in their bleached blond hair to make it spiky, and swirling blue patterns painted on their bodies to intimidate their enemies. Caesar believed fighting the disorganized, quarrelsome British tribes would be a pushover. But he wasn't prepared for the British weather.

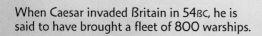

When Caesar invaded Britain in 54BC, he is said to have brought a fleet of 800 warships.

Caesar's crossings

When Caesar made his first crossing to Britain in 55BC, storms drove part of his army back to Gaul. He won some battles in the southeast, but was surprised by the Britons' skilled use of chariots in combat. It was not the easy fight he had expected. Gales wrecked many of his ships on the beaches where they had landed and he was forced to retreat. Caesar returned the next year, but soon had to go back to Gaul to deal with a revolt there.

Internet links

For links to websites where you can see a map of the Roman empire and find out more about the invasion of Britain, go to **www.usborne-quicklinks.com**

British warriors, some on their battle chariots, massed on the cliffs of Kent to watch the Roman army as it approached.

The empire strikes back!

The Romans didn't give up on Britain. In 43, nearly a hundred years later, they invaded again and eventually conquered all but the highlands of Scotland. For the next 400 years, Britain was a part of the mighty Roman empire – its daily life, culture, language and landscape changed forever.

Did you know? In 40, crazy Roman Emperor Caligula wanted to invade Britain. But he stopped at the French coast, where he ordered his men to collect shells to prove his "conquest" of the sea!

TRIBAL BRITONS

W hile the Romans had been busy conquering a vast empire, building magnificent, bustling cities and developing a sophisticated urban culture, the people of Britain were living a simpler rural life.

Internet links

For a link to a website where you can find out what life was like in an Iron Age round house, go to **www.usborne-quicklinks.com**

Iron age living

There were no real towns in Britain before the Romans came, certainly nothing to match the gleaming marble streets of Rome. But some people lived in fortified hilltop settlements, called hillforts. This period in history is known as the Iron Age, because this was when people first began to make tools and weapons out of iron. Iron Age Britons are now famous among historians for their decorative metalwork and for their distinctive dwellings – unlike most Europeans of the time, their houses were round.

A divided land

Although the Romans saw the Britons as a single race, the land was divided into more than 20 separate tribal areas, each made up of several scattered farms and villages. Most tribes had their own king, and relations between them were usually peaceful. Not all of the tribes spoke the same language, but they understood each other, because they used variations of a group of languages, known as Celtic. They traded with other Celtic-speaking peoples in northern Europe, as well as with one another. But they had little sense of belonging to one country.

This reconstructed Iron age village at Butser Ancient Farm, near Chalton in Hampshire, shows what round houses would have looked like.

Round houses didn't have windows, so the doors were built facing east to let in the morning sun.

Did you know? To make their houses weatherproof, the Britons covered the wooden, or *wattle*, walls in *daub* – a mixture of mud or clay, straw and manure.

This helmet, decorated with Celtic designs, is a fine example of British Iron age metalwork.

Tribal conflict

During the early 1st century, a warlike tribe called the Catuvellauni, led by an ambitious chief, Caratacus, began to dominate the southeast of Britain. Gradually, they captured more and more territory from surrounding tribes. Finally, at the beginning of the 40s, Verica, king of another tribe called the Atrebates, fled to Rome and pleaded for help. This gave the Romans the excuse they needed to invade Britain again, picking up where Julius Caesar had left off.

Roman influence

After Caesar's attempted invasions, southern British tribes had much closer contact with the Romans, especially those who traded with Romans in Gaul. Some tribes paid taxes to Rome, in return for the promise of protection and alliance. A few British tribal chiefs were even educated there.

Each house usually consisted of one large room with a fire in the middle for cooking.

There was no chimney in the thatched straw roof, so smoke seeped out through the thatch instead.

CLAUDIUS CONQUERS

From 27BC, the Roman empire was ruled by a series of emperors. In 41, Emperor Caligula was assassinated by members of his own army, who then declared his uncle Claudius the new emperor. To avoid Caligula's fate, Claudius did his best to win the respect and loyalty of his army and his people. When King Verica appealed to Rome for help, Claudius seized his chance. He was determined to prove himself a strong leader by conquering Britain once and for all.

Internet links

For a link to a website where you can see pictures and movies of Roman soldiers in battle, go to **www.usborne-quicklinks.com**

River raids

Claudius ordered a massive 40,000 troops to invade Britain. They landed on the southeast coast and marched inland until they reached a river. Caratacus and his army were waiting on the other side. While both armies prepared for battle, the shrewd Roman general, Plautius, sent a team of crack troops downstream. They swam across the river on horseback, to launch a surprise raid. Meanwhile, the rest of the army crossed the river upstream, unnoticed, and attacked the Britons from behind. It was a decisive Roman victory.

Hillforts were protected by rings of deep ditches and massive earth mounds that could be up to 24m (80ft) high.

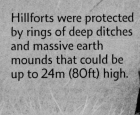

This huge catapult, called a *ballista*, shot boulders and heavy iron-tipped bolts over great distances.

Britons under siege

Next another general, Vespasian, pushed west along the south coast, laying siege to as many as 20 British hillforts. During a siege, the Romans surrounded the fort and subjected it to a merciless missile attack until the Britons were forced to surrender.

Roman archers shot flaming arrows into the hillfort, to burn it down.

Britons hurled rocks at their attackers.

The Romans used a huge battering ram to smash their way into the hillfort.

This smaller catapult, like a crossbow, was called a *scorpio*.

In tortoise, or *testudo*, formation, Roman soldiers used their shields to form a protective shell around them, so they could storm the hillfort, safe from any missiles.

Claiming Colchester

Once most of the south of England was in Roman hands, Vespasian sent for the Emperor. Barely four months after the invasion began, Claudius and his legions marched in to capture the Catuvellauni stronghold of Colchester. Eleven British tribal chiefs came to surrender to Claudius. Just two weeks later, he returned to Rome, to a hero's welcome. There was a triumphal procession through the city to celebrate his conquest of Britannia.

Caratacus in chains

Caratacus ran for his life. In 51, he sought refuge with the Brigantes tribe, in the north of Britain. Their queen promptly handed him over to the Romans. Then he was sent to Rome, where he was paraded through the streets in chains. When he appeared before the Emperor, he is said to have asked, "If you Romans choose to lord it over the world, does that mean that we have to accept slavery?" Claudius was so impressed with his dignity that he decided to spare his life.

 Did you know? When Claudius captured Colchester, his troops included several war elephants. The locals, who had probably never seen such creatures before, must have been terrified.

BATTLING BOUDICCA

Over the next 30 years, the Romans gradually conquered most of Britain, but they often met fierce opposition. To keep order in the province, they got help from the local tribal leaders. If they supported Rome, they were given top jobs and allowed to keep their land. But the Romans soon learned that they couldn't control the British against their will. In 60, they faced an uprising so serious that it nearly spelled the end of Roman rule.

Internet links

For links to a websites where you can read more about Boudicca and her rebels and find out how a Celtic war chariot was built, go to **www.usborne-quicklinks.com**

Trouble brewing

One of the British leaders who was loyal to the Romans was Prasutagus, King of the Iceni tribe in East Anglia. On his deathbed, he divided his kingdom between his daughters and the Roman Emperor. But, when he died, the Roman authorities ignored his wishes, seizing the Iceni lands and all their possessions. When Prasutagus' wife Boudicca protested, she was whipped in the middle of the village and her daughters were raped. The queen was furious – this was war!

As they confronted Roman forces, Boudicca's rebel troops included some women, who fought beside the men.

On the rampage

Boudicca immediately raised a vast rebel army of men, women and children – all keen to drive out the occupying forces. They headed for Colchester, the Roman capital, ransacked the city, killing thousands of people and destroying anything that represented Rome. Then they turned on *Londinium* (London) and *Verulamium* (St. Albans). All three cities were burned to the ground in a ferocious assault.

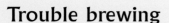 Did you know? Nobody knows what happened to Boudicca after she was defeated, but legends say that she and her daughters poisoned themselves, to avoid being captured by the Romans.

Opposing forces

While this was happening, most of the Roman army in Britain was hundreds of miles away in north Wales, fighting another rebellious group, the Druids. When news of Boudicca's revolt came through, the army rushed back to deal with it. By the time the two armies faced each other for battle, Boudicca's troops far outnumbered the Romans' 10,000. But the Britons stood little chance against the disciplined and heavily armed professional Roman fighters.

War trumpet

The most important warriors rode swiftly around the battlefield on the back of war chariots.

Charge!

At the battle cry, the Britons sounded their war trumpets and charged, full tilt at their opponents. But their front line was struck down by a volley of Roman javelins. Then the Romans advanced in tight formation, with their swords stabbing in front of them from behind their shields. They marched steadily forward, wading through the Britons, who turned and fled.

This British warrior's shield was found in the Thames, at Battersea, in London.

Carnage

The Britons' escape was blocked at the sides by the Roman horsemen. At the back they were hemmed in by their own wagons, where their families had parked to watch the battle. It was a chaotic bloodbath, in which Roman chroniclers claimed 80,000 Britons died.

MILITARY MIGHT

The key to the Romans' success in conquering so much of Britain so quickly was the virtually unstoppable power of their army. Not only was it the largest military force of its time, but its men were the most strictly organized, best equipped and highly trained fighters of the time.

Internet links

For a link to a website where you can find pictures and information about legionaries' clothes and weapons, go to **www.usborne-quicklinks.com**

Organization

At its largest, the Roman army had over 300,000 men. To keep such a vast fighting machine running like clockwork, it had to be strictly regimented. So it was divided into units called legions. Each legion had over 5,000 foot soldiers, or legionaries, organized into groups of 80, known as centuries. With a clear chain of command, every man knew his place and exactly what was expected of him.

The legions were led into battle by officers with banners.

Foreign fighters

At first, only Roman citizens – men born in Rome or Italy – could become legionaries. They made up about half of the army. The rest were non-citizens, recruited from the provinces and known as auxiliaries. When they retired, they became citizens, so their sons were allowed to become legionaries.

The wide crest on this man's helmet means he is a centurion.

A general commanded several legions.

A legate was in charge of a legion.

A centurion led a century (80 men).

A legionary was a citizen foot soldier.

A cavalry soldier fought on horseback.

A non-citizen fighter was called an auxiliary.

A soldier's life

Legionaries were the elite soldiers of Roman times. To be eligible, a man had to be over 17, literate, tall and very fit. In return for 20-26 years' service, a legionary earned a good wage and learned a trade, such as engineering or medicine. If he proved brave and loyal, he could rise up the ranks to become a *centurion*, the officer in command of a century.

Standard issue

When they joined up, all legionaries were issued with a kit that gave them the cutting edge over their enemies. Each man had a short sword, called a *gladius*, a dagger and a spear-like javelin. For protection in battle, legionaries were given a metal breastplate, a helmet and a large, curved shield. They also carried cooking utensils and tools for building temporary battle camps.

Boot camp

Roman soldiers had to be primed and ready for action at any time. So, even in peacetime, they had to follow strict training regimes to keep super fit. As well as perfecting their javelin throwing, swordcraft and tactical moves, they also went on three training marches a month. These involved marching over 30km (18.6 miles) at a rapid pace, in just five hours. Soldiers were expected to train wearing full combat gear and carrying heavy packs. No wonder the average legionary went through three pairs of boots a year!

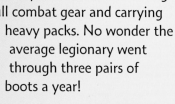

Did you know? Over time, more and more people across the Roman empire were granted citizenship. So by the 3rd century, there was little difference between legionaries and auxiliaries.

KEEPING THE PEACE

Once Roman rule was established in Britain, the role of the army changed from an invading force, to a peacekeeping one. Now its main job was to defend the country against attacks from hostile tribes and to enforce Roman law. But Roman soldiers were more than just fighters; they also had several non-military duties too.

Three legions, from Germany and Gaul, were based in Britain. They lived in fortresses in Caerleon, York and Chester. There were also dozens of smaller auxiliary units in forts across the country – mainly along the frontiers.

The largest forts were almost like small towns, with everything the soldiers needed, from barrack blocks and bathhouses, to hospitals and stables. They all followed the same rectangular plan, with the headquarters in the middle. So men could always find their way around – whether they were in Manchester, Mainz or Mesopotamia.

Internet links

For links to websites where you can take a virtual tour of a Roman fort and find out more about life in the barracks, go to
www.usborne-quicklinks.com

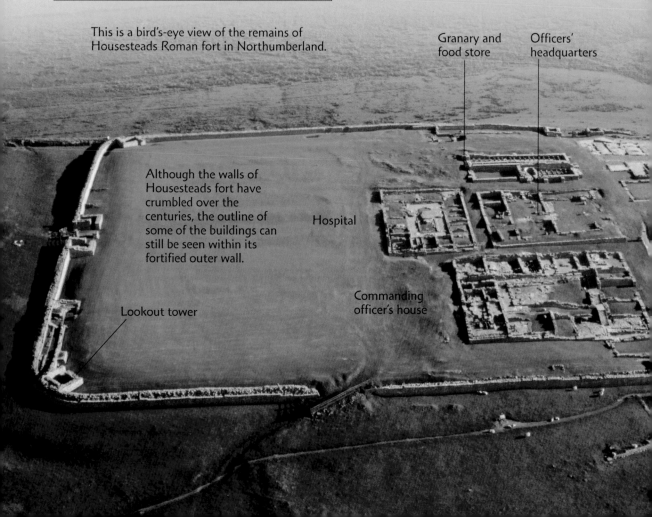

This is a bird's-eye view of the remains of Housesteads Roman fort in Northumberland.

Granary and food store

Officers' headquarters

Although the walls of Housesteads fort have crumbled over the centuries, the outline of some of the buildings can still be seen within its fortified outer wall.

Hospital

Commanding officer's house

Lookout tower

Roadworks

There were no proper roads in Britain before the Romans. So, to link the forts, the army built a brand new network of over 16,000km (1,000miles) of roads. These were vital for governing the province, transporting supplies, moving troops and sending messages. The roads were built to follow the most direct or convenient route possible. So, many were incredibly straight. Several roads in Britain today have been built over the original Roman ones.

This bronze helmet was found at the site of Ribchester Roman fort, in Lancashire.

Romanizing the natives

Many soldiers made friends with the locals, teaching them the Roman way of life, but adopting British customs too. When they retired, they often settled near their old forts, and even married local women. Over time, British and Roman cultures became more and more mixed. Britons could also become "Romanized" by joining the army themselves. For some, this was a chance to travel and experience life in other parts of the empire.

Barrack blocks

Main gateway

Latrines (communal lavatories)

Letters home

In the ruins of the Roman fort at *Vindolanda* (Chesterholm), archaeologists have found hundreds of written records, which paint a detailed picture of the daily lives of soldiers in Britain. Among them are duty rosters that describe soldiers working as shoemakers, brewers, builders and medics. The soldiers' own letters include party invitations, deals with local traders and even a letter from a mother sending underpants and socks from home.

This is a razor handle, shaped to look like a legionary's leg. If you look closely, you'll see the thick, patterned socks, worn under the sandals.

Did you know? Many British towns that grew on the sites of Roman forts – Manchester, Colchester, Gloucester and Leicester – have name endings derived from *castra*, the Latin for fort.

TOWN LIFE

If Britain was to become a fully fledged part of the Roman empire, then its people would have to learn how to live and think like Romans. To the Romans, the only civilized way to live was in a town – but the Britons didn't have any. So the Romans got building.

This scene shows the bustling market square, or *forum*, of the Roman town of Caerwent, in south Wales.

Like the forts, every Roman town followed a similar design. The streets were laid out in a grid, dividing the town into rectangular blocks known as *insulae*. At the heart of every town was the *forum*, a busy market square where people met to do business and catch up on the news. The *forum* was lined with shops on three sides, and on the fourth side stood the Roman equivalent of the town hall, the *basilica*.

The town council held its meetings in this building, the *basilica*.

British temple

Town houses

A wealthy Roman would have lived in a large, luxurious town house, or *domus*. But most people lived in the *insulae*, working in various trades and services. They sold their wares – from metalwork and pottery, to meat and bread – from shops at the front of their houses and lived at the back or upstairs.

Public conveniences

Fresh water was supplied to towns through a system of pipes called aqueducts. Most people didn't have water at home. They collected drinking water from wells or fountains in the streets and used public toilets and bathhouses. People had to pay to use the lavatories, so many used buckets at home, which they simply emptied into the gutters!

In this aerial reconstruction of Roman Caerwent, you can see the grid pattern of roads, with the forum in the middle and the town wall around the outside.

Defending towns

Roman Britain was usually a peaceful place, but during the 2nd century many towns had fortified walls built around them. These were not just for protection; they were also a way to show off a town's importance. More importantly, the walls enabled soldiers to control the traffic going in and out, making sure that traders paid their taxes on goods bought and sold.

Town councils

The Romans divided most of Britain along tribal lines, into regions called *civitates*. Each had a main town (or civitas capital) with a council of local leaders in charge of taxes, law, public buildings and roads. By involving the Britons in local government, the Romans hoped to keep them loyal and avoid rebellions.

—— Roman temple

Internet links

For links to websites where you can see a virtual reconstruction of a room in a *domus* and find out more about life in a Romano-British town, go to **www.usborne-quicklinks.com**

Did you know? Colchester, York, Lincoln and Gloucester were built to house Roman army veterans. Known as *coloniae*, they served as regional capitals, run by Roman officials.

BATHTIME

The focus of social life in every Romano-British town was its public bathhouse, which consisted of a series of rooms of different temperatures. There, for a small fee, people could scrub and scrape, pamper and preen, and wash away the cares of the day. They could also work out in the exercise yard, unwind with a massage or catch up on the gossip over a game of dice.

Internet links

For a link to a website where you can find out more about Roman Bath and play a baths game, go to **www.usborne-quicklinks.com**

Scrubbing up

Before the Romans, Britons washed with soap, but the Romans preferred to use perfumed oil instead. Before taking a bath, they rubbed the oil into their skin, then they lifted weights and did their exercises. Once they had worked up a sweat, they scraped off the oil, sweat and grime, using a curved tool, called a *strigil*. Then, they were ready to take a dip.

Many wealthy people, like the man seated here, paid slaves to do their scrubbing and scraping for them.

Taking the plunge

The bathing ritual usually began with a dip in a tepid pool in a room known as the *tepidarium*. The bather then moved to the steamy *calderium* to soak in a hot tub. The routine was finished with a refreshing swim in the cold, outdoor pool or *frigidarium*.

Did you know? After their baths, people could play board games, buy snacks from food stalls or listen to musicians and storytellers – it's no wonder they spent so much time at the baths!

Aquae Sulis

One of the most magnificent bathhouses in Roman Britain was in the spa town of Aquae Sulis (now called Bath), where cleanliness and godliness came together. Long before Roman times, Britons had visited its sacred hot spring to worship Sulis, the water goddess of healing and wisdom. The Romans linked Sulis with their own goddess, Minerva, who also had healing powers. So they built a temple by the sacred spring and dedicated it to Sulis-Minerva.

Roman dice found in a bathhouse in London

The Roman baths at Bath can still be seen today, although much of the building was rebuilt in the 19th century.

Bath's baths

Later, a large bathhouse was added to the temple, using the naturally heated water from the spring. People visited from all over Europe, making Bath one of the most lively and holy towns in Roman Britain.

The water from the spring at Bath comes out of the ground so hot that in this photograph, you can see the steam rising from it.

LONDINIUM

London didn't exist before the Romans came to Britain; it was no more than a few farms scattered along the River Thames. But when Claudius invaded in 43, his men built a bridge across the river and put up a fort to guard it. Soon, local traders and craftsmen settled near the fort and a town grew up on the north bank of the river.

The Thames was wider than it is today and deep enough for ships to sail right up to the bridge, where a port was built. This made the river a useful trading link between Britain and the rest of the empire. Within ten years, London – which the Romans called *Londinium* – had established itself as a thriving, cosmopolitan merchant town.

This is an artist's impression of London in 120. Most of the city grew up on the north bank of the river Thames, but a small trading settlement also developed on the south bank.

The area occupied by Londinium is now the financial district of modern London, known as "the City".

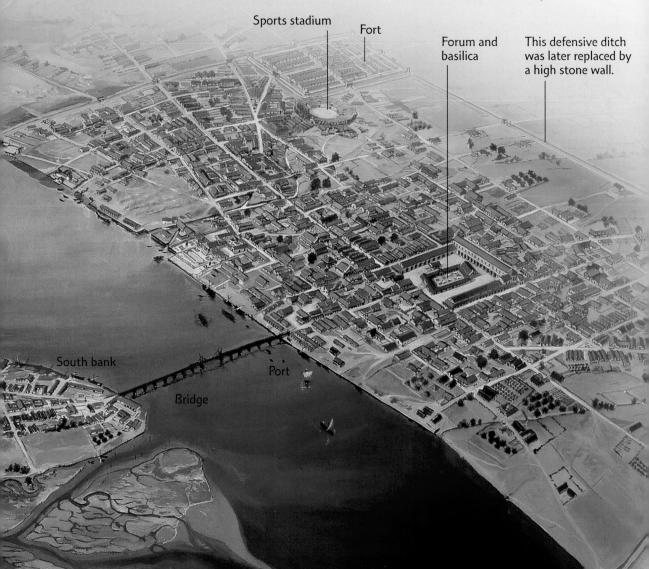

Sports stadium

Fort

Forum and basilica

This defensive ditch was later replaced by a high stone wall.

South bank

Bridge

Port

This model shows Londinium port and the Roman bridge across the Thames.

Britain's first capital

Another town that grew rapidly during the early days of Roman rule in Britain was Colchester. In 49, the Romans had made it into a *colonia*, a town for Roman settlers and ex-soldiers. It soon became the first capital of the Roman province of Britain. Then, in 60, Colchester and London were burned to the ground by Boudicca and her rebels. Both towns were quickly rebuilt, but Colchester's old tribal connections made it politically unstable. London, sited on the Thames, was more convenient for trade and transportation. So, gradually the Romans moved their headquarters to London.

Internet links

For a link to a website where you can take a trip back in time to visit Londinium, go to **www.usborne-quicklinks.com**

Imperial London

By the turn of the 1st century, building work had begun to transform London into an imperial city, boasting a grand basilica and a forum larger than Trafalgar Square. Later, an imposing city wall was added, to defend the capital. At the heart of commercial and political life in Britain, London flourished and became one of the great cities of the Roman empire.

Power base

A few emperors did visit Britain, but most of the time the province was run by a governing council, based in London. It was led by a governor, who was head of the army and chief justice. To make sure he didn't become too powerful, the emperor appointed another official, called a procurator, to collect taxes and control the country's finances.

Did you know? The Roman bridge across the Thames is no longer standing, but it crossed the river at almost the same point as London Bridge does today.

MARKET FORCES

The new Romanized lifestyle in Britain led to an industrial boom, as craftsmen and merchants rushed to meet people's demand for new products. The new road system boosted local trade, making it easier to move goods around the country than ever before. International trade also flourished, as British products could now be transported as far away as Syria or Africa, in exchange for exotic foreign produce. The Roman empire soon became one great marketplace.

All at sea

The Romans had a vast fleet of merchant ships to transport goods around the empire. Roman sailors didn't have instruments to help them to navigate the seas. So they judged their position by the sun, moon and stars, and consulted books which recorded the best routes and times to travel. To guide ships safely into dock, the Romans built lighthouses at key ports, such as Dover.

This map shows where different goods came from around the empire. Roman lands are shaded green.

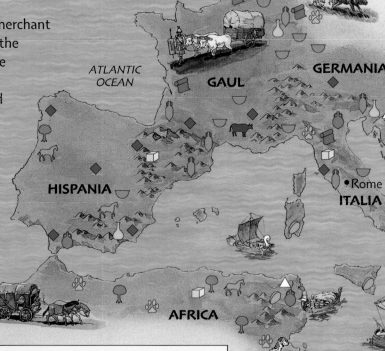

Grain	Pottery	Purple dye
Olive oil	Metals	Hunting dogs
Wine	Glass	Cattle
Salt	Wood	Horses
Cloth	Marble	Wild animals

Checks and balances

Fair trade depended on standard weights and measures throughout the empire. Roman merchants weighed their goods with a scale called a steelyard (see right). Legionaries regularly inspected the weights used in the markets to make sure that customers weren't being cheated by unscrupulous traders.

To use a Roman steelyard, like this one, merchants hung their goods from hooks on one side.

Then, they slid a weight along the arm until both sides balanced. Notches on the top told the weight of the goods.

Internet links

For a link to a website where you can read about the life of a Roman merchant and other traders, go to **www.usborne-quicklinks.com**

BLACK SEA

ASIA

CYPRUS

SYRIA

MEDITERRANEAN SEA

ARABIA

EGYPT

Made in Britain

One of the main reasons why the Romans invaded Britain was for the silver, gold, copper, tin, iron and lead mined there. These were used to make all kinds of things, from coins and fancy metalwork, to army helmets and pipes for plumbing. Industries, such as pottery and the wool trade, also grew under the Romans. Most British goods were sold locally, but some were exported. One of the most prized British exports was a hooded cloak called a *Birrus Britannicus*.

Luxury imports

Many of the ingredients essential to the diet of any civilized Roman – wine, olive oil and fish sauce – weren't made in Britain. So they were shipped over from Spain and Italy, stored in tall pottery jars called *amphorae*. Other luxury goods brought to Britain included glossy red pottery from France, fine glass from Germany and Italy, and rich perfumes and spices from Egypt and the Middle East.

Did you know? The same money was used all over the Roman empire. This made trade between different provinces much easier and more fair than if they all had different currencies.

FASHIONABLE SOCIETY

Romano-British society had a strict pecking order, which showed in the way people dressed. Slaves, who didn't count as citizens and had no rights, wore very simple clothing, and ordinary citizens dressed little better than their slaves. But people with wealth and power liked to flaunt it, adorning themselves with the finest fabrics and the most glittering gems.

Wardrobe essentials

Whatever their age, sex or social status, all Romano-Britons wore a basic garment called a tunic. It was made from two rectangles or T-shapes of woollen or linen cloth, sewn at the sides and shoulders, often tied around the waist with a belt or cord.

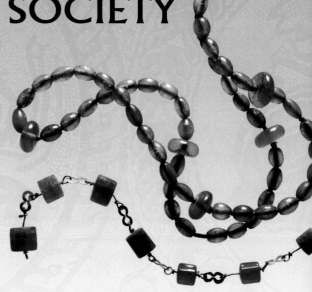

These Roman necklaces are made from amber, emeralds and gold.

Celtic chic

Before the Romans came along, the Britons had their own distinctive style. The Romans tended to wear plain clothes in sober shades, but the Britons liked bold stripes and plaids, in as many gaudy shades of russet, yellow, blue and purple as possible. They decorated their clothes with embroidered designs and fastened them with large, decorative brooches and belt buckles. Under Roman influence, fashion-conscious Britons began to dress more like their new rulers, but they kept some of their native style too, adding Celtic touches to Roman outfits.

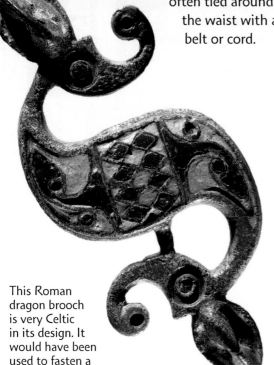

This Roman dragon brooch is very Celtic in its design. It would have been used to fasten a person's cloak.

Internet links

For links to websites where you can see more pictures of Roman fashions, go to **www.usborne-quicklinks.com**

 Did you know? While many Romano-Britons went barefoot, most people wore leather sandals. In colder parts of the country, they even wore their sandals with thick socks!

Accessorizing

Men and women all piled on as many jewels, brooches, necklaces, rings and bracelets as they could afford. These showed a person's wealth and could be made from anything, from wood and bone to gold and silver. Brooches and pins weren't just fashion statements; they were also the best way to keep your clothes on!

Gold doesn't tarnish, so these rings are as shiny now as when they were new.

Power dressing

For formal events, men wore a *toga*, a large semicircle of cloth, draped carefully over the tunic. *Togas* were complicated to put on and so heavy that men had to walk very slowly in them. This looked dignified, but it wasn't very practical, so *togas* were usually only worn by rich men. A man's *toga* reflected his status. Most men wore an undyed toga, magistrates or politicians were allowed to wear one with a purple band, but only the emperor could dress all in purple.

The purple stripe on this man's *toga* shows that he is a magistrate.

The head of this bone hairpin (shown at actual size) has a hairstyle that was the height of fashion in the 1st century.

Hairdressing

The Roman emperor and his wife, the empress, set the trends right across the empire. Under Roman rule, men were usually clean-shaven and cut their hair short. But when Emperor Hadrian was depicted on a coin wearing a full beard, many men copied his style. Women's hairstyles usually involved sweeping long hair into a bun. Slave girls spent hours styling their mistresses' hair in more and more elaborate buns, sometimes using hair pieces, decorated with hairpins and piles of false curls.

The woman having her hair done wears a dress called a *stola* over her tunic.

SPORTS AND SPECTACLES

To keep their subjects happy and loyal, Roman emperors and officials put on spectacular public shows in every town. These entertainments were often staged as part of public holidays or religious festivals and included plays and chariot races. But most popular of all were the sensational, often very violent, sporting shows, known simply as "the games".

The games were held in a large stadium on the edge of town, often with enough seats for the entire local population. A day at the games began with a grand procession of all the performers around the oval arena. This was followed by animal fights, mock hunts, wrestling matches, public executions and finally gladiator combats. If there was an army base nearby, the arena also hosted military displays and mock battles.

Caerleon Amphitheatre, in South Wales, provided enough seating for an audience of 6,000. This is how it may have looked during the 2nd century.

Special guests, including local politicians and maybe even the emperor himself, sat in an enclosed seating area, where they enjoyed the best views of the games.

Gladiators

The highlight of the games was undoubtedly the gladiator combats. Gladiators were slaves or prisoners, specially trained to fight. Gladiators, equipped with different weapons and costumes, were pitted against each other, and sometimes against animals. They were the superstars of Roman times. If they won enough contests, they could win their freedom. But it was a brutal and bloody sport; gladiators were expected to fight to the death.

Drama queens

Theatrical shows were another popular form of public enertainment in Roman times. Plays known as tragedies told classical tales of the gods, while comedies were about ordinary people and could often be very rude. To compete with the thrill of the games, these dramatic performances included all kinds of special effects, music, dancing and sometimes very realistic violence.

This mosaic is from Rudston villa, near Hull. The chariot racer is waving a palm leaf, showing he won.

A day at the races

The Britons were skilled in the use of chariots in warfare, so they probably relished the Roman sport of chariot racing. Racers hurtled around a large track at breakneck speeds, crashing into one another to try to throw their rivals off course. The worst collisions – known as shipwrecks – were often fatal. But the violence wasn't limited to the racetrack. Charioteers raced in teams and brawls often broke out between fans of opposing sides.

Outside the main arena, people could buy snacks and trinkets or watch other entertainers.

Internet links

For a link to a website where you can dress a gladiator and choose his weapons to see how he succeeds in combat, go to **www.usborne-quicklinks.com**

 Did you know? The games were so gory that huge vats of incense had to be burned in the arena to cover up the smell of all the blood.

HADRIAN'S WALL

The Romans originally intended to keep extending their territory in Britain until they had conquered the whole island. But in 117 there was a new Roman emperor, Hadrian, and he had other plans. He spent more than two thirds of his rule in the provinces and believed it was more important for the Romans to strengthen and defend the land they already had, than to conquer new territories. In 122, he visited Britain, where he set his ideas in stone.

This head is all that's left of a statue of Hadrian, that once stood at about 2m (6.5ft) tall. It was erected in London in around 122.

At the end of the 1st century, a Roman governor named Julius Agricola captured some land in Scotland, which the Romans called Caledonia. But the local people weren't easy to conquer and the Romans were often attacked by hostile Caledonian tribes. So they gradually withdrew their troops and Hadrian ordered a fortified frontier wall to be built, to protect Roman Britain. This allowed the army to control who crossed the border. It was also a potent symbol of the power of Rome.

Much of Hadrian's Wall still snakes its way across the north of England today.

Internet links

For links to websites where you can find out about life along Hadrian's Wall and in Scotland during Roman times, go to **www.usborne-quicklinks.com**

Stonewalling

Hadrian's Wall was the largest structure in the Roman empire and an impressive feat of engineering. It was 120km (75 miles) long, stretching right across the country between the the Rivers Tyne and Solway. Along the wall there were sixteen forts, with smaller forts called milecastles, every Roman mile in between. There were also lookout turrets so soldiers could keep watch for trouble and pass messages between forts.

Antoninus in Scotland

Within months of Hadrian's death in 138, his successor, Antoninus Pius, attacked Scotland again. By 142, he had captured southern Scotland so he began building a new frontier wall across the country. The "Antonine Wall" was about half the length of Hadrian's and was mostly built from blocks of turf, instead of stone. But, less than 20 years later, local tribes rebelled, forcing the Romans back behind Hadrian's Wall. This remained the northern frontier for the next 250 years.

At its largest, Hadrian's Wall, was was over 4.5m (15ft) high and 3m (10ft) thick.

Did you know? Romans measured distances by the number of strides taken by legionaries on the march. 1,000 paces, left and right, made a Roman mile, about 1,500m (just less than a modern mile).

GODS AND GODDESSES

The official Roman religion was made up of many gods and goddesses. As long as the Britons worshipped the Roman gods, they were free to follow as many other religions as they liked. So, they kept their own local gods alongside Roman ones, as well as adopting exotic cults from far-flung corners of the empire. With so many foreign influences, Britain became a religious melting pot.

This is what the temple to the Emperor Claudius in Colchester, would have looked like before it was destroyed by Boudicca's army.

Most of the Roman gods and goddesses were adopted from the Greeks, but given Roman names. Each one was said to control a different aspect of life. The king of the gods was Jupiter, based on the Greek god Zeus. People prayed to Mars for success in war, to Minerva for wisdom and to Venus for love. Many emperors were declared gods when they died. Statues and temples to past emperors were built all over the empire.
Praying to them was a mark of respect for the Roman rulers.

Most of the time, only priests were allowed inside Roman temples.

Mix 'n' match religions

Like the Romans, the Britons worshipped a number of gods and goddesses. Many Roman settlers adopted the local gods, often matching them to Roman gods with similar characteristics. Over time, the identities of these mix 'n' match gods became blurred. New ones emerged, combining aspects of native and Roman gods.

This is part of a bronze sculpture of Sulis-Minerva, found at Bath. Her identity combined Sulis, a local water nymph, and Minerva, a Roman goddess.

Sacred rituals

Religious rituals took place at temples that housed statues of the gods. On a holy day there was a procession of priests and musicians playing on pipes and tambourines. When they reached the temple, an animal – oxen, goats and chickens were common offerings – was sacrificed on an altar outside. Other, simpler gifts the people made to the gods included cakes, wine and money.

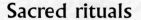

Sacred rituals took place at this altar.

Exotic cults

Roman soldiers came to Britain from all corners of the empire, bringing their religions with them. These included devotion to mother goddesses, such as Isis from Egypt and Cybele from Turkey. Mithras, the Persian god of light, was particularly popular with soldiers and merchants, because he stood for discipline and fair play. Only men could worship Mithras. They met in underground temples, where they underwent all kinds of gruesome initiation rituals, including being locked in a tomb for several hours.

Internet links

For links to websites where you can read stories about the Roman gods and explore a reconstructed temple of Mithras, go to **www.usborne-quicklinks.com**

Did you know? The Romans accepted the Britons' religion, but not their priests, the Druids. In 60, the legions stormed Anglesey, the Druids' holy island, and killed almost all of them.

EARLY CHRISTIANS

Gradually, many people began to lose faith in the state gods and goddesses. Instead, they turned to new religions that had been brought to Britain by Roman soldiers from the Middle East. The most popular was Christianity. Unlike previous religions, this new faith had strict rules on how its followers should live, and offered them life after death.

Internet links

For a link to a website where you can find out more about how Christianity spread throughout the empire, go to **www.usborne-quicklinks.com**

The first Christians

Christianity began about 2,000 years ago when a Jew named Jesus started preaching in Judea, a small Roman province in the Middle East. After he died, his followers continued to teach his ideas. By the end of the 2nd century, Christianity had spread right across the Roman empire to Britain.

Secret worship

The Romans banned this new religion and persecuted Christians throughout the empire, because they refused to worship the Roman emperor or the state gods. Christians risked flogging, imprisonment and even execution if they were caught. Despite the dangers, many Christians continued to meet and worship in secret. Some of them even set aside a room in their home to use as a church.

House church

Wall paintings

Altar

This is a reconstruction of Lullingstone Roman villa, in Kent, cut away so that you can see the the house church inside.

The cellar housed what historians think was a pre-Christian shrine.

People often decorated their house churches with mosaics and wall paintings of religious images and symbols.

 Did you know? Around the end of the 4th century, a Romano-Briton named Patrick sailed to Ireland to preach Christian teaching. Later, he became St. Patrick, the patron saint of Ireland.

These painted figures, from the house church at Lullingstone, show how early Christians prayed with their arms outstretched, not with their hands together.

Dying for the cause

In the early 3rd century, the first Romano-Briton is thought to have died for his faith. He was a soldier named Albanus, who was beheaded after giving shelter to a Christian priest who was fleeing persecution. Many years later, Albanus was made a saint and his town, *Verulamium*, was renamed St. Albans. The most brutal persecution took place a century later, when Emperor Diocletian ordered the deaths of thousands of Christians across the Roman empire.

This mosaic (from Hinton-St-Mary Roman villa) is the oldest picture of Jesus Christ in Britain. The letters behind him are a Christian symbol, called the chi-rho. They are the first two letters of Christ's name in Greek: chi and rho.

A Christian emperor

In 306, there was a new emperor, Constantine, who was sympathetic to Christians and ended the persecution. Later, he even became a Christian himself. Gradually, the religion gained more and more followers, and in 391, the emperor Theodosius declared Christianity the official Roman faith. Although some people still believed in the old gods, their worship became illegal and many old temples were turned into churches.

33

COUNTRY LIFE

After the Romans arrived, dozens of new towns and army forts were built around Britain. The thousands of people who lived there didn't produce their own food. But the new road network made it much easier and quicker for farmers to transport their produce to these new consumers. For the first time, farming became big business.

Farming innovations

To supply the growing demand, agriculture became more intensive. Farmers began to rotate their crops – planting a field with corn one year and beans the next – to keep the soil rich. The Romans developed more efficient tools and brought new ideas about fertilizers, land drainage and animal breeding.

Grand designs

As farms grew, so did the houses where the successful farmers lived. Soon after the Roman invasion, many of them began to adopt a more Roman lifestyle. They replaced their round houses with rectangular huts, which they rebuilt in the Roman style, adding extra floors, verandahs and annexes as they grew wealthier. By the late 2nd century, many of these farmhouses had become lavish mansions, which the Romans called *villas*.

This scene shows how a Romano-British farm estate would have looked in the 2nd century.

A palatial villa, like the one on this hilltop, would have belonged to an exceptionally wealthy family.

Some fields were left "fallow" in alternate years to rest the soil.

Social changes

Before Roman times, Britain's farmland was divided into small farms, owned and farmed by individual families and tribes. But, as farming became more commercial, many wealthy landowners bought up huge estates. The peasants no longer owned their own land, but rented homes on the estate they farmed. This social system lasted in England and Wales for the next thousand years, long into the Middle Ages.

The chase

Hunting was central to country life in Roman Britain, both as a sport and for catching food. Animals hunted included hare, deer and wild boar, but hunting for birds was also popular. In fact, it was the Romans who first brought pheasants to Britain, especially to hunt. Hunters used a variety of weapons including bows and arrows and spears. This was a great privilege: all other civilians were strictly forbidden from carrying weapons.

This is a mosaic of a hunter, from Chedworth Roman villa. He has caught a hare and seems to be carrying a stag's antler.

Pigeons were kept to use as food during the winter.

These are beehives. The Romans used honey to sweeten their food.

Oxen were used to pull heavy machinery.

Hens and ducks were kept for their eggs and meat.

Did you know? The Romans introduced the Britons to many new vegetables, including cabbages, carrots, lettuce and onions. Before then, they mainly ate bread, stews and porridge.

HOME COMFORTS

Whether they lived in a sprawling *villa* in the countryside or a large *domus* in town, Roman Britain's rich and famous lived in houses that were luxurious, even by today's standards. For men, such as government officials and merchants, it was important that their homes reflected their wealth and status. So they had opulent living rooms, stylish dining rooms and formal courtyard gardens.

Internet links

For links to websites where you can find a selection of tasty Roman recipes, and take a virtual tour of a Roman villa, go to **www.usborne-quicklinks.com**

Home entertainments

Wealthy Romans loved to show off their beautiful homes by throwing extravagent dinner parties that lasted long into the night. The meal opened with appetizers such as salads, eggs, oysters and sardines. For the main course, fish, meat and poultry were served, often with strong sauces made from fish or spiced fruit. This was followed by fruit, nuts and honey cakes, all washed down with plenty of wine.

Music and dancing

Hosts often hired musicians to entertain their dinner guests. Some rich Romans did learn how to play musical instruments, but they thought it was undignified to play in public. So most professional musicians and dancers were slaves. The instruments they played included pipes, lyres (small harps) and tambourines.

This scene shows a fashionable dinner party in full swing. Romans usually ate with their fingers, reclining on couches.

Home decorating

Even grand Roman houses looked plain on the outside, but they were lavishly decorated inside. The walls were plastered, then painted with bright patterns or pictures. Sometimes, these wall paintings included fake columns and marble effects. The floors were decorated too, with mosaics – designs made from thousands of tiny tiles.

All mod cons

While most people lived without, the finest homes in Roman Britain were fitted with running water, toilets and sometimes their own bathhouses. Many also had a central heating system, called a *hypocaust*. Furnaces were fired in the cellar, so warm air flowed under the floors and through ducts between the walls. This would have been a must for Romans from warmer provinces, who would have found Britain a chilly place.

Lyre

Tambourine

Pipes

Warm air duct

The Romans called wall paintings frescos.

Furnace

The floor has been cut away here so you can see the hypocaust system underneath.

Tiled floors were often decorated with designs.

The floor is raised on pillars to allow hot air to circulate.

 Did you know? In Roman times, larks (tiny birds) were considered a great delicacy. A popular dish was marinated larks' tongues – it took about 1,000 birds to make the recipe.

FAMILY AFFAIRS

In the days before the Romans came, it was possible for some British women, like Boudicca, to hold leading positions in society. But, under Roman rule, a woman's place was far more limited to the home, where she was expected to look after the family. A typical Romano-British household was made up of the head of the family – known as the *paterfamilias* – his wife and children and his sons' wives and children. It was a father's duty to lead the rituals that marked the most important events in family life: births, deaths and marriages.

Myrtle was often used to make wedding garlands.

Making a match

When a Romano-British girl was about 13, her family arranged a marriage for her, choosing a man with a similar or slightly better position in society. Wedding customs varied a lot in Roman times, but some British families adopted the Roman way of getting married. On the morning of a typical Roman wedding, the bride dressed in a long white tunic with a saffron-yellow veil, or *flammeum*, over her head. Then the family decked the house in ribbons and garlands of flowers.

Wedding vows

When the groom and the guests arrived, a priest sacrificed an animal to the gods, so that they would bless the marriage. After signing the marriage contract, the bride and groom joined their right hands to say their vows. The ceremony was followed by a feast and a torchlit procession to the groom's house. There, the bride was carried over the threshold, into the arms of her new husband and the couple began married life.

During a Roman wedding ceremony, a *pronuba* (usually the matron of the house or the bride's mother) presided over the hand-holding ritual.

When a child is born

A wife's main duty was to produce lots of children – preferably boys who might bring prosperity to the family. Childbirth was a risky business in Roman times, and shrouded in mystery. During pregnancy, women prayed to the gods for safe delivery of a healthy baby. When a baby was born, it was placed at the feet of the *paterfamilias*, who lifted it up as a sign that he welcomed it into the family. At nine days old, the baby was named and given a lucky charm, or *bulla*, to ward off evil spirits.

In sickness and in health

In Roman times, people knew little about how the body works or what causes diseases. Most doctors worked for the army and could only perform very basic operations. So, if a member of the family fell ill, he or she was usually treated by a friend with a little knowledge of herbal remedies. Many people thought sickness was a punishment from the gods. So they tried to find a cure by chanting spells or praying to gods with healing powers.

When a body was cremated, the ashes were often buried in a pot, like this one decorated with a face.

Until death do us part

When a person died, the family chanted a mourning song while the body was washed, annointed with perfumed oils and clothed. For the funeral, the body was carried to the cemetery, outside the town walls, followed by mourners and musicians. The Romano-Britons believed in life after death, so people were often buried with things they might need in the afterlife, such as money, shoes or the tools of their trade.

Fennel was supposed to calm the nerves.

Sage was used in cough mixtures.

Lemon balm was believed to cure headaches.

Internet links

For a link to a website where you can examine the contents of a Romano-British doctor's grave, go to **www.usborne-quicklinks.com**

Did you know? Couples chose their wedding date carefully to avoid a day that might bring them bad luck. June was considered a lucky month, so most weddings took place then.

GROWING UP

Being a child in Roman times probably wasn't much fun, because as soon as they were old enough, most boys were sent to work. Their sisters stayed at home to learn how to spin wool, weave, sew and cook. But, if the family could afford it, at the age of seven, boys and a few girls were sent to a school called a *ludus*.

A teacher was called a *pedagogus*. Many of them were slaves from Greece.

Ancient learning

Before the Romans, the Britons taught their children by word of mouth, passing on stories, poems and songs about the heroic deeds of their ancestors. Instead of writing these stories down, they learned them all by heart. As they didn't keep written records, British scholars, such as the Druids, were able to keep their learning and ideas secret from outsiders.

Older students read works of history and literature from scrolls.

Text messages

But, after the Romans arrived, teaching was based on writing, rather than the spoken word. Paper hadn't been invented yet, so there weren't any books. Instead, children read the works of Roman and Greek authors from large scrolls, made from papyrus reeds. They wrote out their lessons using a pointed tool, called a *stylus*, to scratch words onto a wooden tablet coated with wax. Once the tablet was full, pupils used the flat end of the *stylus* to smooth the wax out, ready to start again. Older children sometimes wrote on thin sheets of wood, using metal pens dipped in ink.

Pupils wrote out their lessons on wax tablets.

They did their sums using a counting frame called an abacus.

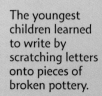

The youngest children learned to write by scratching letters onto pieces of broken pottery.

  Did you know? At the age of 13 or 14, a boy officially became a man. He was given a toga to wear, had his first shave and was registered to vote. Then his family held a party to celebrate.

Great expectations

Most children finished school at age 11. But boys from affluent families went on to advanced studies at a school called a *grammaticus*. There, they were groomed for high-flying careers in law or politics. Their lessons included Greek and Roman literature, history, geography and mathematics. Another important subject was public speaking, or *rhetoric*, which the Romans considered a crucial skill for any official job.

The word

To be successful in Roman times, the Britons didn't just need to learn how to read and write; they also had to learn a new language. Lessons were taught in Latin, the official Roman language of government, law, the army, business and trade. In the towns, younger people picked up Latin and passed it on to their children, but Celtic was still the common language at home and in rural areas.

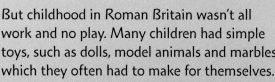

Marbles and games pieces were made from glass, bone or pottery.

Child's play

But childhood in Roman Britain wasn't all work and no play. Many children had simple toys, such as dolls, model animals and marbles, which they often had to make for themselves. They also played games that would be familiar today, including dice, board games, hide-and-seek, ball games and hopscotch.

Internet links

For a link to a website where you can find out how to play some of the ball games Romano-British children may have played, go to **www.usborne-quicklinks.com**

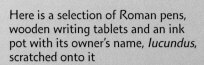

Here is a selection of Roman pens, wooden writing tablets and an ink pot with its owner's name, *Iucundus*, scratched onto it

RULING BRITANNIA

For nearly 150 years after Boudicca, the Romans ruled Britain with very little opposition. But, near the end of the 2nd century, Roman power became weakened by political turmoil back in Rome, as rivals competed to become emperor. Over the next century, a series of rebels took advantage of the chaos to seize power in Britain for themselves.

Divide and rule

In 192, Emperor Commodus was assassinated. Civil war broke out in the empire, as legions from different Roman provinces each proclaimed their own leader as the new emperor. One of them was the British governor, Clodius Albinus. But, eventually he was beaten to the top job by Septimius Severus, a general from Africa. To prevent future governors from becoming too powerful, Severus split Britain into two smaller provinces: *Britannia Superior* and *Britannia Inferior*. They had a governor each, based in London and York.

Rebel empire

After Severus died, the empire was plunged into civil war again. The fighting went on for fifty years and became known as the Anarchy. During this turbulent period, Britain, Gaul, Spain and lower Germany broke away to form an independent Gallic empire. It lasted 14 years until 273, when a strong new emperor, Aurelian, brought the provinces back under Roman control.

Emperor Septimius Severus with his family

Minted

During the Anarchy, steep price rises and high taxes drove some people to forge counterfeit coins. Aurelian made reforms to prevent this. Like many Roman emperors, he also used the coinage to boost his public image. Every coin showed his portrait on one side and publicized his latest achievements on the other. This showed the people who was boss and kept them up-to-date with the news.

This gold coin shows Aurelian on the front and celebrates his victory over rebel provinces on the back.

Saxon pirates

Near the end of the 3rd century, tribesmen from northern Germany, called Saxons, launched a number of pirate raids in the North Sea. To protect themselves, the Romano-Britons built a string of heavily defended forts along the southeast coast. They called it the Saxon shore. Compared to normal Roman forts, the Saxon shore forts varied a lot – some were oval or even multi-sided in shape – their walls were higher and thicker, and they had more lookout towers.

Internet links

For a link to a website where you can find a timeline of the Roman occupation of Britain, go to **www.usborne-quicklinks.com**

The "British emperor"

Carausius was the Roman admiral in charge of a fleet in the channel and responsible for building some of the Saxon shore forts. In 286, he was accused of keeping some of the Saxon pirates' bounty for himself. To avoid being punished, he seized control of Britain and proclaimed himself Emperor.

While the Saxon shore forts kept the Saxons out, they probably helped Carausius to fend off the Romans too, for a while. His independant British empire held out for ten years – until the Romans invaded and recaptured Britain. This time, the Romans divided the land into four provinces, with new capitals at Cirencester and Lincoln.

Portchester castle, near Portsmouth, is one of the Saxon shore forts built by Carausius in the 280s.

The fort is so big that another castle (in the bottom left corner) and a priory church were built inside the original Roman walls, during the 12th century.

Did you know? During the Anarchy, there were more than 20 Roman emperors in just fifty years – and almost all of them met a violent death.

ARTS AND CRAFTS

Wealthy Romano-Britons loved to fill their homes with beautiful things. They paid highly-skilled craftsmen to produce an enormous variety of mosaics, sculptures, and beautiful artifacts that we can still admire today.

Internet links

For a link to a website where you can make a mosaic online, go to **www.usborne-quicklinks.com**

Artistic differences

Artistic styles in Roman Britain combined two very different traditions. The British style was usually abstract, with intricate curved patterns and spirals. But the Romans liked to depict the gods, people and nature. Under Roman influence, British craftsmen began to illustrate the same subjects as the Romans, but often using a more decorative style.

Marvellous mosaics

Mosaic floors were often laid in grand homes and public buildings. Designs ranged from geometric patterns and borders, to elaborate scenes from ancient myths – made up of thousands of tiny tiles, or *tesserae*, set in concrete. Complex designs were put together in wooden frames in the craftsmen's workshops. These were set in position, then simpler sections were completed on site.

This floor mosaic, from Bignor Roman villa, in Sussex, shows Venus.

Sculpture

There were all kinds of different uses for sculptures in Roman Britain. Government officials employed skilled sculptors to produce grand, larger-than-life statues of Roman emperors and dramatic carved battle scenes to grace town squares and public buildings. At the market, people could buy small mass-produced statuettes of gods for their shrines at home. Other sculptors applied their art to decorating people's gravestones with pictures of them at work or with their families.

This large silver dish is the most prized piece of the Mildenhall treasure. It shows the sea god, Neptune, surrounded by dancers and mythical creatures.

Gorgeous glass

By the 1st century, the Romans had learned how to blow and shape molten glass to make anything from a simple jar to an exquisite drinking goblet. Plain glass bottles were manufactured cheaply in bulk. Precious glass objects could be tinted, engraved or even gilded. They were used at elegant dinner parties or put in people's graves as funeral offerings.

This blown glass flagon was discovered in a Roman grave, in Buckinghamshire.

Buried treasure

In the 1940s, a farmer in Mildenhall, Sussex, was digging his field when he discovered a spectacular hoard of Roman silverware. This is one of a number of treasure troves in Britain, that were buried near the end of the 4th century. It is possible that its owners were burying their most valuable possessions for safekeeping, in case they were stolen by Saxon raiders. We don't know what happened to the people, but they never retrieved their treasure. So it remained intact and undiscovered for over 1,500 years.

 Did you know? The most successful mosaicists had large workshops, where they passed on their skills to apprentices. Many also had their own signature styles, patterns and subjects.

DECLINE AND FALL

By the end of the 4th century, Roman power over western Europe was starting to decline. A succession of weak emperors and attacks on the frontiers had taken their toll. So the Romans began to take troops out of Britain to defend other places. Even the city of Rome was under threat. Four centuries of Roman rule in Britain finally came to an end.

Boom and bust

Despite the turmoil elsewhere, the first half of the 4th century was a time of peace and prosperity in Roman Britain. This was when many of the most lavish villas were built and British craftsmen were producing some of the finest mosaics and most elaborate pieces of metalwork. But the Roman system was beginning to crumble. Gradually, more and more people were leaving the towns to live in the country, and once-grand public buildings were falling into disrepair.

End of an era

By the beginning of the 5th century, the Saxons had intensified their raids in the south. The north was also under increasing attack, from tribes from Ireland and Scotland (Caledonians and Picts) breaking through Hadrian's Wall. In 410, Rome itself was overrun by Germanic tribes. The emperor, Honorius, told Britain it would have to fend for itself.

Regime change

Roman rule was over, but the Roman way of life went on in parts of Britain for the next 150 years. In the north and west, many people continued to live as they had before the Romans, keeping the Celtic language and culture alive. But, during the 5th and 6th centuries, southern Britain came under new influences, as Saxons, Angles and Jutes (Germanic tribes) settled and formed their own kingdoms. It was the beginning of a new age for Britain.

This painting shows a gang of Saxon raiders attacking a Romano-British walled city.

 Did you know? The period of British history that followed Roman rule is sometimes known as the "Dark Ages" because it seemed comparatively uncivilized and less was written about it.

ACKNOWLEDGEMENTS

Every effort has been made to trace the copyright holders of material in this book. If any rights have been omitted, the publishers offer their sincere apologies and will rectify this in any subsequent editions, following notification. The publishers are grateful to the following individuals and organizations for their permission to reproduce material on the following pages (t = top, b = bottom, l = left, r = right);

Cover, main image © Jeff Morgan/Alamy; **background** © Adam Woolfitt/CORBIS; **back cover** © John Russell; **End papers, p1, 24-25, 30-31, 44-45, 46-47,** © HIP/CMDixon; **3 (br)** © John Martin/Alamy; **6-7** © Butser Ancient Farm, www.butser.org.uk; **7 (tl)** © The British Museum/HIP; **12-13** © Charles and Josette Lenars/CORBIS; **14-15** © Skyscan; **15 (tr)** © The British Museum/HIP; **15 (br)** © Philippa Walton/The Portable Antiquities Scheme, with thanks to Bob Middlemass and Rolfe Mitchinson; **16-17** © National Museums & Galleries of Wales; **17 (tr)** © National Museums & Galleries of Wales; **18-19** © Jon Eisberg/Getty Images; **19 (t)** © Museum of London/HIP; **20** © Museum of London; **21 (t)** © Museum of London; **23 (tr)** © The British Museum/HIP; **24 (tr)** © Museum of London/Bridgeman Art Library; **24 (bl)** © The Trustees of The British Museum; **25 (r)** ©Museum of London/HIP; **25 (t)** © The British Museum/HIP; **27 (tr)** © Hull and East Riding Museum, Humberside/Bridgeman Art Library; **28 (bl)** © The Trustees of The British Museum; **28-29** © Adam Woolfitt/CORBIS; **31 (tr)** © R. Sheridan/Ancient Art and Architecture Collection; **32** © Peter Dunn/English Heritage; **33 (tr)** © Crown copyright. NMR; **33 (tr)** © HIP/CM Dixon; **33 (t)** © Ancient Art and Architecture Collection; **33 (tl)** © HIP/CM Dixon; **35 (tr)** © Topfoto.co.uk PAL; **39 (tr)** © National Museums & Galleries of Wales; **41** © The British Museum/HIP; **42 (b)** © The Trustees of The British Museum; **42 (tr)** © Staatliche Museen, Berlin/ Bridgeman Art Library; **43 (b)** © Skyscan; **44** © Ancient Art and Architecture Collection; **45 (tr)** © The British Museum/HIP; **45 (bl)** © The Trustees of The British Museum; **46** (b) © Museum of London/HIP

Additional illustrations by Inklink Firenze and Ian Jackson
Cartography, for picture map of Roman Britain, by Craig Asquith
Cover design by Zoe Wray
Photoshop by John Russell
Design assistance by Katarina Dragoslavic

INDEX